Gods
8000 years ago

Darwin is wrong !
There are people in the universe like humans

Stephane Baillon

STEPHANE BAILLON

Copyright Stephane Baillon 2023

Darwin is wrong! We are not evolutionarily descended from the ape. In fact, there are people in the universe who are physically exactly similar to us humans.

How do I know that ?
Because these people, physically exactly like us humans, traveling in a spaceship, by accident, crashed on our planet 8000 years ago and we called them "gods".

Here is their story

CHAPTER 1

Crash

8000 years ago, a huge spacecraft carrying 200 individuals entered our solar system. Obviously they had no choice but to crash on Earth.

The exact place where they crashed is called "Soker" called today Sakkara, Egypt, 25 km (15 miles) south of the city of Cairo and the Pyramids.

They crashed in the middle of the desert of Egypt.

The spacecraft must have taken very heavy damage as they were unable to immediately get going again. Like us humans would have done, they built a wall all around the spaceship to protect it.

A wall surrounding the spaceship

This wall is 10 meters (32 feet) high and it is 550 meters (600 yard) long by 275 (300) wide, which must have corresponded to the size of the spacecraft. Seen from above.

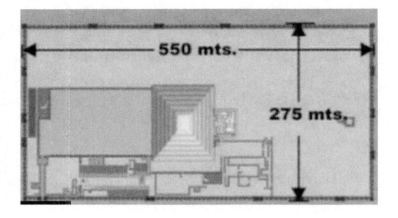

The spacecraft had to take up all the space.

After his departure, the Egyptians will keep the wall and Imhotep will build this pyramid in the center.

This spacecraft had to be huge, gigantic. Twice as tall and twice as wide as today's largest cargo ship, twice as tall and as wide as today's huge cruise ships.

The size of this spacecraft, stranded in the sands of Sakkara, must have been immense.

The gigantic spacecraft must have been black with rounded parts and more angular parts because Egyptian humans of the time who saw this spacecraft compared it to a giant beetle.

The Egyptians reproduced the shape of this black and gigantic vessel which was to exceed from the protective wall.

Or again like that (exhibited in the museum of Turin, Italy).

Beneath the immense spaceship, in the basements of Sakkara, were built, 28 meters (92 feet) deep, in a perfectly mathematical way, a sophisticated underground network composed of 15 rooms, 15 chambers, with tunnels aligned in a mathematical order, all in complex mathematical geometry.

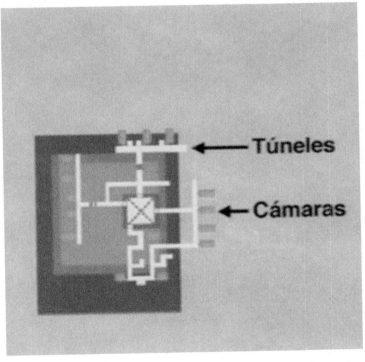

To lead to this vast underground network, a 50 square meter (538 sq ft) lift was built from the surface descending directly to the underground. This well is 7 meters (23 feet) long and 7 meters

(23 feet) wide, or 49 square meters (538 sq ft).

This elevator, as big as an apartment, must certainly have had the function of raising and lowering goods and people from the surface, from the ship, to the 15 underground rooms at 28 meters (92 feet) deep in this vast underground network that they created.

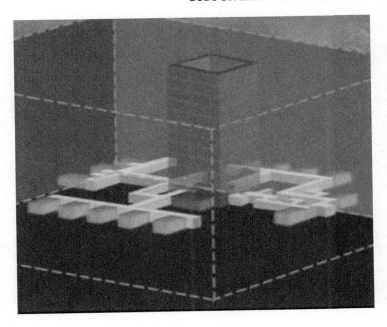

To allow underground ventilation, a complex and sophisticated ventilation system was dug into the rock to capture air from the surface.

CHAPTER 2

Like humans

The Egyptian humans saw these individuals who were in this spaceship.

A closer look reveals a pilot in the eye of the spacecraft.

Individuals came out of this spaceship and the Egyptians described them on the walls of their temple.

They really looked like humans.

There were men and women but no children in this spacecraft. Only adults.

Men have exactly the same physical characteristics as male humans namely a head with hair, arms, trunk, legs, feet with five toes. Two hands with five fingers on each hand.
They are also the same size as humans. They are not taller or shorter than humans, the same size.

Drawing by Champollion 1850

The women of this vessel that comes from space are also exactly similar to human women with long hair too and breasts on their chests. Same female body shape thinner than male. Same hips, same legs, same beauty as human women.

Drawing by Champollion 1850

CHAPTER 3

Flying boats

These individuals who have built a wall all around their spacecraft move through the air using small spaceships that can carry multiple individuals.

These vessels are described by the Egyptians of this time as flying boats.

They carry several of these humanoid beings.

These aliens travel through the air all over Earth with small spaceships.

Presumably they are looking for materials to repair their spacecraft and energy to start engines again.

But, this search is going to take a long, very long time. So long that humans will age and die before the ship is repaired and these aliens who physically look like us are stuck on Earth for many years.

Humans observe these humanoid people who do not age unlike us humans. They always remain the same, men and women, they are immortal, time does not affect them. It is like if their cellular system did not get old like us human.

Humans call them "GODS".

CHAPTER 4

Advanced genetic modification

These people who came from space using a spacecraft have much more advanced technology than we do today.

Their technology allows them to know the composition of each plant, each stone, each soil, each sea. They also know the biological composition of the animals and insects that live on this planet but also that of humans.

These foreigners know human beings perfectly. They have records on humans. Our physical composition, the structure of our bones, our muscles.

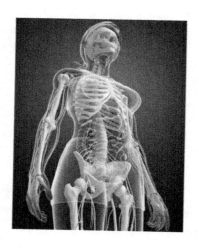

Files on our Complete Anatomy

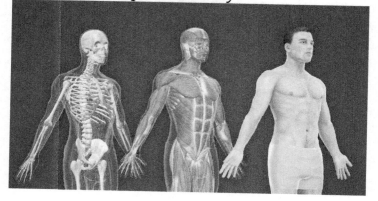

The level of our intelligence

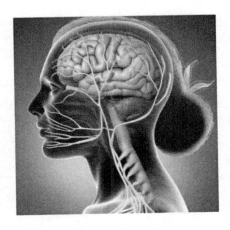

And our intellectual abilities.

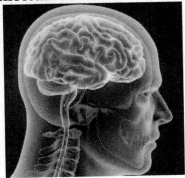

This planet is what we would call a "Colony".

A planet on which tests have been carried out for a long time, for a million years.

We find traces of these first attempts with the dating of Lucy, this first biped considered as the first evolution of the human.

This will be followed, for a million years, by regular visits by scientists from space to observe evolution and to carry out genetic modifications or even new tests because the results did not seem satisfactory for them because these monkeys evolved but not satisfactory have been eliminated and no longer exist today.

This is how we find traces, skeletons and skulls of these hybrid beings between humans and monkeys everywhere on Earth for a million years but who have all disappeared and none has survived.

Darwin's theory establishes that animals on earth evolve in their environment, but evolution is different for humans. No other species on Earth that has evolved has had their brains increased in size. Only this hybrid species between humans and monkeys has seen its brain develop artificially. The development was done in successive stages, like steps of stairs, because at each stage there was an external non-earthly intervention. This is why human scientists fail to understand how Homo Sapiens, the modern man, that we are today, appeared 100,000 years ago.

We haven't evolved from this homo sapiens species. Our brain hasn't evolved or grown for 100,000 years. We are exactly the same today as humans were 2,000 years ago, 5,000 years ago, 20,000 years ago, 100,000 years ago.

We have the same physical characteristics as the Greeks of 2500 years ago or the Egyptians of 5000 years ago. The same brain, the same way of thinking. There is no evolution. Only an optimized diet makes modern populations ever so slightly taller, but that's it. We won't get taller or smarter.

100,000 years ago, people from space created this human man and woman.

Some physical differences such as skin color depending on the climate but we, humans, are all exactly the same in every continent everywhere on Earth. Same intelligence, same way of thinking. Inside, we are all exactly the same. Outside, only a few minor physical differences.

CHAPTER 5

Humans are carnivores

These aliens from space, stranded by accident on this Earth, know humans. They have files on us homo sapiens humans.

I think they were forbidden to come and run aground on this colony but they had no other choice. In reality, the arrival of these beings, by accident, on Earth, created an upheaval that superior forces in the universe did not want.

On their files, it was clearly indicated that humans were animals, wild beasts. Humans are animals that eat fruits but also and especially the meat of other animals after killing them.

Humans are carnivores and eat everything in an animal: muscles, organs like liver, kidneys, heart of another animal. It also eats the brains, eyes, and tongues of other animals. The human eats everything that is possible in another animal, even the inside of the bones, leaving only what is really indigestible to him like the fur or the bones.

At first, these foreigners are wary of these humans, these wild beasts capable of killing everything that lives for food.
Even though these aliens have eternal life, they are not immortal and they have the same organs

as humans located in the same places. So these foreigners are wary of these wild beasts that look like them physically which is misleading.

These aliens are afraid that humans will try to kill them to eat them because that's what we, humans, do.

When I was younger, I watched a series called "V". This series showed beings from outer space, in spaceships that looked nice but were monsters inside that ate live rats.

In reality, it's the opposite, it's us, humans, the monsters who eat other animals, even raw.
These foreigners are vegetarians.

After a period of observation of humans, the gods realize that humans are hungry and kill for food like the majority of animals on Earth.

These strangers, these humanoid aliens, have a chief, a leader. A man called the "king of gods" or the "god of gods".
Humans called him also in a lot of mythologies the "god of the sun" because a strong light seems to go out of him. Some kind of natural lighting.

After many years, the gods were unable to take off,

to make their spaceship refilled with energy, it is as if there was not the energy they need on this planet . So, stuck on this planet, the king of gods began to communicate with humans.

The gods observe the humans who look so much like them and who live in difficult living conditions, constantly torn by hunger.

These aliens from space are going to take pity on the harsh and precarious living conditions of the Egyptian humans who live next to the spaceship and who are hungry too all the time. So, the king of gods does something totally new, he helps humans not to be hungry anymore.

The gods have a very sophisticated technological equipment, a knowledge, a very great knowledge and they know the chemical composition of each element on Earth, each plant. Being vegetarians themselves, they teach Egyptian humans how to feed themselves other than by hunting, fishing, gathering and they teach them agriculture, the cultivation of wheat, this plant which, once harvested, can be kept all year round and once crushed, allows the production of bread.

The gods know that the chemical composition of bread allows the human organism to live and bread, agriculture, will represent an essential stage in the development of humans. The basis of human food becomes bread.

The gods who help the Egyptians help all other people on Earth who are also suffering from hunger and gods teach them too agriculture, farming.

They teach humans to nourish their bodies with plants. It will be wheat almost everywhere in Europe, Egypt and Mesopotamia.

But also rice in Asia because it is easier to grow in moist soil.

but very nutritious for humans too.

And corn on the American continent.

A food as nutritious as wheat or rice.

CHAPTER 6

Unexpected

Humans who eat well and are no longer hungry surprise the gods with their reaction.

Humans thank the gods and show a strong devotion and a very strong love for them. A bit like an animal is grateful if a human helps it but even stronger because it is about humans.

The gods are surprised by this unexpected reaction which is not marked on their files about humans.
In the end, humans don't only think about killing and eating, they are able of reflection and gratitude. It's not marked on their human files.

The king of gods, the god of gods, the sun god, decides to share more knowledge with humans even though he knows it is forbidden.

He teaches humans to use plants to dress, to

heal. These foreigners know all the compositions of each plant and the benefits of each plant on humans.

Humans are very receptive to knowledge. This receptive side of humans to knowledge is not listed on their file either.
The human turns out to be much smarter than indicated on files about humans.

For these aliens from outer space, humans are unable of thinking. Just as we, humans, think that animals are unable to think similarly to us humans.

On their files, humans look physically exactly like them, gods, but humans come from a cross between this humanoid race and the animals present on Earth.
The human is a hybrid being. In this last biological manipulation done on this planet 100,000 years ago, homo sapiens looks a lot like the gods but with a much less intelligent brain and with a lot of animal chromosomes inside him. Nevertheless, the physical similarity is amazingly so close. Humans look like exactly as gods physically.

But, this planet Earth is very special and this new hybrid species called human is much more surprising than what is written on their files. It is the king of gods, seeing this specificity who will make first a rapprochement, a communication, with humans.

For some unexplained reason, the king of the gods, the god of gods, is going to be amazed at the human abilities and this tremendous alchemy that has happened on this planet.

While this is strictly forbidden by higher forces under heavy penalties, the King of Gods is going to help humans everywhere on Earth. Not only does he teach them knowledge and knowledge, but he explains to them how to evolve even further. It's as if he knew humans are very close to something special, very strong, unique in the universe.

Humans show a great intelligence to keep knowledge because, despite the fact that they are mortal, they manage easily, with poems, songs, traditions, to transfer all the knowledge to the following generations.

After food, the manufacture of clothes, the king of the gods teaches humans the alloy of metals for the manufacture of cauldrons. Always to allow humans to eat and nourish themselves better.

This is Gundesprut silver cauldron dug in Denmark 1891. The god woman, the god man with beard and the king of god are sculpted on it.

For the king of the gods, food should not be an obstacle. The human must dedicate himself to something bigger, higher, more spiritual.

CHAPTER 7

The three gods

To give all humans a chance, the king of the gods travels the entire planet by air using a small spaceship to bring this same knowledge to all the peoples he meets.

In all the mythologies throughout the world, the king of the gods is always described as a man of great physical beauty.

He is often accompanied by two other gods, each on a small spaceship.

There is a woman with long black hair.

With a sword in her hands

and a stocky, hulking man who has a white beard and white hair but he is not old.

They travel using small spaceships.

All the peoples on Earth thus evolve at the same time.

Everywhere, in all the tribes they encounter, the gods give knowledge freely without asking anything in return. They give agriculture, eat with plants, heal with plants, dress with plants. Then, they leave and promise to come back with more knowledge soon.

The knowledge changes the lives of humans so much in comfort and freedom from hunger that humans look forward to the return of the gods.

And the gods indeed always return by the air to bring always more knowledge.

Humans worship the gods because after each visit, their living condition improves further.

After agriculture, the gods teach humans the many uses of milk from other animals for making cheese and the benefits of this milk for young children. But also the use of metal and the use of the wheel.

Humans are so grateful that they love the gods very much. These beings who come to meet them by air, who give all this very useful knowledge with an immediate effect on the well-being of the village and who save the children.

Then, without asking for anything in return, these beings, with perfect male and female physiques, set off again on their spaceships in the sky.

Obviously, this knowledge is so wonderful that

humans worship the gods and look forward to their return.

The gods receive this love from humans and it touches them very much. Humans have this exceptional ability to love unconditionally and the gods appreciate it very much.

Everywhere on Earth we begin to draw the king of the gods, the god of the gods who turns out to be a man of exceptional physical beauty.

Humans also draw those who accompany him, this woman of great beauty with straight black hair. The Japanese make her their main deity. She had to look like them physically.

Humans also draw this powerful man with white hair and white beard.

His memory is found in Santa Claus who comes to bring, on a flying chariot, precious presents, knowledge for a more pleasant life.

A man with a white beard who brings useful gifts, knowledge.

CHAPTER 8

Worshiped

The gods are beings with such strong knowledge that diseases and epidemics disappear when they arrive in a village.

These journeys of the gods to give knowledge to humans will last a long time, between 1000 and 2000 years. The gods go on world tours whenever they find useful knowledge for humans. The gods even explain to humans the effects of other planets on Earth.

They are superior beings adored everywhere on Earth for this knowledge which they bring freely, without asking anything in return.

All people across the earth speak of these people, these gods who bring knowledge.

The Dogons in Africa proudly display the

representation of the gods in their rites.

And their celebrations

The knowledge of the gods remained in this Dogon people for 8000 years. In 1930, a French scientist, showing great humility and respecting these people a lot, was accepted among this Dogon population who agreed to share very ancient knowledge with this scientist.

The Dogons knew Sirius B in 1930 before being discovered in 1974 thanks to a new modern telescope.

Humans, everywhere on Earth, have drawn the image of the gods and especially that of the king of the gods, the being called by all mythologies "the perfect being".

A man of exceptional physical beauty. He had black, wavy hair.

His facial features were as fine as a woman's. He had perfect masculine musculature with harmonious proportions.

He is represented by the Greeks as the perfect and powerful Apollo, king of the gods.

His friends called Athena.

And Zeus.

One might think that Zeus is the most important deity of the Greek pantheon but no, the temples dedicated to Apollo are the most numerous.

CHAPTER 9

E pluribus unum

All the mythologies around the world are interesting because each of the human peoples has managed to keep a part, a piece of this memory of the gods traveling everywhere on Earth and giving all the tribes knowledge. But, two mythologies have better kept the details of these gods.

These two mythologies are in one part Egyptian mythology.

Egypt, where the giant spaceship crashed. Egypt is the headquarters of gods.

But another mythology is also very interesting and perhaps gives even more details about these beings from another world, it is Indian mythology.

Indian mythology describes these gods, their life, battles and a lot of details on the king of gods, the god of gods, the handsome god.

Through a simultaneous study of these two mythologies, we have many details about these beings, these gods from elsewhere, who are so close to us physically.

These mythologies also give many details about the other gods who accompanied the king of the gods, the god of the gods, the perfect being, on the starship.

Already, we can see that they are a lot. There are many gods.

In Egypt.

In India

Lot of people

They were moving on a spaceship that could carry 5-7 people.

These vessels flying in the sky are flying boats in Egypt carrying many people.

Or just one person

They are those flying spaceships in India.

CHAPTER 10

Others people in universe

There must be many colonies in the universe because in this shipwrecked, many people have different skin colors. It's not uniform. It ranges from light to dark skin like on our planet but there are also other skin tones that we do not know on Earth.

If we compare the two mythologies, Indian mythology and Egyptian mythology, we can assume that the vast majority of these beings have light skin, but there are also dark skin people like on Earth.

The details of the different skin colors among these foreigners are well drawn on Egyptian walls.

A light-skinned woman and behind her a dark-skinned man like on Earth.

But also a drawing of two women, one with light skin and the other with darker skin.

But also three men, the middle one has darker skin.

Or again here always engraved on the Egyptian walls a man at the top of Denderah roof, a light skin man and one with dark skin.

On the flying starship, five light-skinned people and one dark-skinned woman.

These skin color differences are well described in Egyptian drawing as the country itself is cosmopolitan with variations in skin color.

This is the same for India, where mythology describes many men and women with beige skin color.

With stories and battles.

but also with darker skin too.

There is everything too. There are beards, mustaches, others without beards.

But also women with long black hair and beige skin too.

But, contrary to what is found on Earth, in Egypt and India there are descriptions of men and women with green, red and blue skin color.

In Egypt this black-skinned woman and next to her a green-skinned man. (Sorry for the holders of paper books the cost of the color was too expensive but know that the man behind the woman is drawn by the Egyptians of green skin color).

In India a man with green skin color too. (For paper book holders, it is the man just after the one with the head of an elephant, the skin of this man was drawn green by the Indians).

In Egypt, a man with red skin color. We can clearly see on the Egyptian walls these skin colors much more pronounced than on Earth.

In this image, we can clearly see on the right the woman with light skin, in the middle the man with red skin, like copper, as detailed in Egyptian mythology and this man on the left, seated, who has blue skin.

By the way, this seated man with blue skin is Amon-ra, the king of the gods, the god of the gods, the perfect man.

All Egyptian temples describe his blue skin color which is totally unknown on Earth.

And this woman often with him who has dark hair and light skin.

Once again, unfortunately on the black and white paper books you cannot distinguish the very special blue color of this man called Amon ra or Osiris. However, a simple search on the internet will allow you to find him without difficulty.

This man, the king of gods, the god of gods is depicted with the same blue skin color in India as well.

A particular blue skin color, never seen on Earth.

Once again, and this will be the last image mentioning skin colors, for paper book holders, the skin color of this man called Vishnu or Shiva in India has the specificity of being blue.

CHAPTER 11

Technologic clothes

Thanks to Egyptian and Indian mythologies we have a very good description of these humanoids who look so much like humans and what they wear.

Already, men are drawn half-naked from the torso in Egypt.

Exactly the same descriptions in India.

The king of the gods, like the other gods, wears a rather high helmet which shines in a sparkling yellow light.

These people also have yellow bracelets at the two wrists and at the top of the arms which shines with a strong yellow light.

They also have a large luminous necklace around the neck which covers a large part of their chest. These details are easily visible on Egyptian walls as well as on Indian designs.

All the gods have this very technological equipment and this high helmet while their head is exactly like ours. Their brains don't go any higher. The helmet must be very technological.

They are half-naked and have only one garment that covers their private parts from the waist to the knees. They don't even have shoes.

Women have exactly the same technological equipment, the very high helmet, the bracelets on the wrists and at the top of the arms, the wide necklace on the upper part of the torso.

The difference with men is that women have long hair and a female body with breasts.

Often, women have on the head either a helmet or a kind of tiara in the hair of silver and luminous color which has the same technical characteristics as the helmets of the men. This tiara must be very technological too.

Men have helmets too, sometimes with the visor covering their face, other times with the visor open showing their face.

CHAPTER 12

Snakes

But, all the gods, all the beings that come out of this spaceship are not all exactly like us in human form. Many drawings on Egyptian walls and in Indian mythology describe other beings in the spaceship.

In the first place there is what we could call their pets which accompany gods. Most of them are snakes.

From where these aliens who look like us come from, there are snakes. These snakes are domesticated and protect the gods.

In Egypt on the helmets of the gods, there is always a cobra.

Even several snakes are on the helmet of the king of gods in Egypt.

The snake is major among these people from another world. Snakes help gods and protect them. Snakes are domesticated and live among the gods.

Here are some drawings that are certainly primary but show the importance of snakes among these people of foreigners.

These snakes help the gods

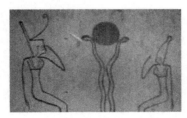

They are among the gods without representing any threat, quite the opposite, they protect the gods. They are pets of the gods.

Look at this picture. On the upper part. The feather symbolizing flying, snakes are symbolized by the Egyptians as flying in the air pulling a kind of chariot on which a person is seated.

Many sculptures of these snakes are of a substantial size. These snakes can be big and tall.

In India also, the snake is major among the people of the gods especially the king of the gods who is, according to Indian mythology, protected by these snakes.

Even in Greece the snake are with the gods, as with Athena.

This legend of the snake which is the domestic animal of the gods is in every mythology everywhere on Earth.

The serpent is with Adam and Eve according to the ancient writings. But, it is also described in many mythologies which speak of the gods with snakes throughout the whole planet.

Here is a representation of Huitzilopochtli, the sun god of Aztec mythology in South America. The same blue skin man as in Egypt (Amon ra) and India (Vishnu) and still protected by this serpent.

No legend describes them as dangerous or attacking, but their presence is very clear among the gods.

This is why in India there are many snake

charmers. The snakes that we find very difficult to domesticate are domesticated pets for these people from another planet.

CHAPTER 13

Lions

In addition to the snake, there is another clearly identified animal which is part of the starship and which is also a domestic animal, it is a lion. This animal follows a woman in Egypt, the black-haired woman.

This same woman on her lion is found very clearly in Indian mythology.

She is described as a formidable warrior riding her lion.

This woman with her lion is also represented in Europe.

In Germany, on this giant sculpture.

And on many monuments in all European capitals.

We also find this woman in Asia, China and Japan also on her lion.

And many statues of Guanyin and Kannon, riding her lion in whole Asia, China and Japan.

This lion may be accompanied by another lion as there are two giant lions carved at the entrance to the Forbidden City in Beijing.

In Europe, these lions mysteriously have wings as if they were able to fly.

According to European legends, two lions pull the flying chariot of the goddess Demeter, the goddess of wheat. Well represented by this sculpture of Demeter and her two lions in Madrid, Spain.

Front view

We also find the legend of the chariot of the goddess pulled by two lions, two lynxs, in Scandinavian mythology. This woman warrior is called Freya, a Valkyrie, a terrific warrior.

CHAPTER 14

Lot of unusual beings

But, there are not only humanoid beings and pets in this vessel of the gods, there are also other hybrid, genetically modified beings.

There are ape men inside this spaceship. Half ape, half humanoid beings.

Egyptian mythology describes these humanoid apes on its walls.

Tall enough ape-men

But it is Indian mythology which is the most precise, the most accurate, on this point. Indian mythology describes several hybrid beings between humans and apes with an ape morphology and a half human and half ape face. Their intelligence must be great nevertheless because they are part of the gods. The ape man spoken of in Indian mythology is called "Hanuman". A monkey-man face, a sturdier human body and a tail.

Indian mythology gives importance on these ape men in their mythology. These ape men are clearly identified as a specific species.

The Indians describe the monkey man helping the beautiful and perfect king of the gods, the blue-skinned man.

In addition to the ape men drawn several times in Indian mythology showing that there were several of them, with the drawings of the Indians we can also see many other half animal, half human beings.

The same goes for Egyptian mythology which describes the heads of several gods with rather special heads, as if coming from a cross with other animals but with a humanoid body.

This is very interesting because it means that there are probably other planets in the universe where there are also animals like on Earth.

These half-ape, half-man hybrid beings don't come from our planet, so they must have come from another planet where the same kind of cellular modification was performed on apes with their humanoid DNA.

This must have given rise to a kind of highly intelligent ape-man.

They must have done the same with other animals on other planets because there are all these strange beings with a clear humanoid body but not the head, an animal head.

In Egypt there is this curious bird man, a male human body, with rather large wings in the back and a face somewhat like an animal.

We find this same character with the same characteristics in Mesopotamia.

Then again the same character in Indian mythology as if he was half bird half human.

In the universe there must then exist birds also elsewhere on other planets.

Cellular modification is common in the universe and among these aliens as there are also drawn beings that we do not know on Earth. There are those beings with the body of a man or a woman with a strange head but also, at the opposite, other beings with an animal body and a humanoid head that we find throughout this area that starts from the Egypt to spread in Mesopotamia to India and also on the other side to Greece.

A sphinx, a lion's body and a woman's face.

STEPHANE BAILLON

This lion's body with a woman's head.

Oedipus and the Sphynx by Francois-emile Ehrmann in 1903

Still other sphinxes with wings.

That can be found everywhere in Europe on many buildings.

Obviously, humanoid beings in the universe are interbreeding with other species just as we do with animals and genetic but even stronger.

This strange being, animal body but with a humanoid head.

Also found in Egyptian temples.

Also in the papyri

The Greeks also describe in their legends and mythologies this animal with a lion's body, wings and a woman's face, but also a woman's chest. Only people capable of genetic modification can be able to create such a creature.

Gustave Moreau, like many painters, will draw this strange animal with a woman's head.

CHAPTER 15

*What about humans
and gods*

Unlike those other planets where half animal half humanoid beings come from, on Earth, a strange alchemy has taken place because we physically look exactly like gods, totally humanoid beings. It is in our genes and our brain that the animal part has remained.

Maybe that's why the king of the gods, the god of the gods, the perfect being transgressed their laws by teaching knowledge to humans. Maybe he had never seen such alchemy in other planets and he decided to teach knowledge even if he had no right to do so.

As the gods communicated with humans for a long time and helped them for a long time, mythologies give us valuable information about these people, because being so close to the gods, humans began to know more about them.

Humans have the ability to domesticate some animals on earth but not the most wild ones.

The gods are superior to us because they have the ability to domesticate and communicate with all animals on Earth, even the wildest ones.

The gods do not have sexual relationships like humans or animals. They are immortal and they are asexual. Men and women look like us but they don't have, or no longer have, the primary animal needed to reproduce like us humans.

There are no children among these people, reproduction is even impossible for them. The organs are on their body but unusable. It doesn't work anymore. Both for men and women.

They have the same physical characteristics as us, humans, but there are some differences besides immortality.

They are smarter than us. Let's say that the most intelligent humans on Earth could reach their level, the thing is possible but is an exception.

They are faster and their physical strength is greater than ours.

Their skin is harder and more resistant than ours and they tolerate the cold better than us. Some Scandinavian legends describe these half-naked gods in the snow and extreme cold when we needed thick animal skins to keep from freezing to death.

That's also why they don't need shoes. Their tougher skin under the feet is not as sensitive as us, humans.

For them, humans are physically and psychologically weak. Humans are for them like a hybrid being between them and an animal.

The gods don't have the need for territoriality like we, humans, have. They don't understand why we fight for a piece of land or a piece of the ocean as if it could be ours. The notion of territoriality as it is written in our genes does not exist for them. Marking territory and fighting for a piece of land, they don't understand. Our animal part, they don't have it.

Nevertheless, the king of the gods, the god of the gods, the perfect being, sees something special in the human that he has never seen elsewhere in the universe.

CHAPTER 16

*Are humans unique
in the universe?*

From my research through all the mythologies in the world, I would say that two things about humans really fascinated the king of the gods, the god of the gods.

The gods appreciate in us humans the fact of loving in this very special way. We love very much. We love in a strong way. Animals love, but humans can love even more. The gods also love but still, humans love even more. Moreover, humans can sacrifice themselves to save other humans for love without an ounce of regret. This very strong ability to love and this feeling of sacrifice for love for others is very widespread among humans.

This very strong love in humans impresses the gods.

This love so strong between humans will even

make the gods a little bit jealous.

Indeed, according to Egyptian and Indian mythologies, two of the gods, the handsome god, the perfect king of the gods, and the very beautiful woman god with long, black hair are so close to humans that a mimicry will occur.

By dint of seeing these human couples love each other so strongly and in such a beautiful way, it will make them want too.

Eventually, even if it must be forbidden to them in the universe, the handsome god man and the beautiful black hair woman god...get married.

They become a couple like humans on Earth.

This notion of a couple is absolutely new and almost unthinkable from where they come from. Seems like that's not done in-universe. It is as if getting married is unthinkable in the universe.

The handsome god and the beautiful goddess marry together. They become a couple. Husband and wife.

In Egyptian mythology like in Indian mythology it is clearly indicated that these two gods are first considered as brother and sister before becoming husband and wife.

This fact is clearly written in Egyptian mythology and in India mythology. The two gods became husband and wife.

This will make humans want to do the same.

Humans begin to marry too.

The first marriages take place in Egypt and India to imitate the two beautiful gods, so perfect, who represent the paroxysm, the ideal of humans. An extremely handsome, strong, very clever man marries the most beautiful of women, a strong warrior, very clever woman.

The gods do not feel the desire for reproduction that we humans feel but, even in the absence of a sexual act, they want to imitate humans in this love so strong that binds two individuals.

Except for the king of the gods and this black-haired woman, the other gods are not going to pair up, and are not going to get married. Only the handsome king of the gods and this beautiful warrior woman are really interested in testing this strong love like humans who fascinates them.

The other point that the gods greatly appreciate in humans is their creativity. Humans are able to create incredible things.
Humans can make useful objects but they also make them useful and beautiful.
The king of the gods, the beautiful and perfect god of the gods, once again, sees something strong in humans that does not exist elsewhere in the universe : creativity.
The handsome god, the king of the gods, teaches humans about music through the learning of the flute and the harp and humans begin to, naturally,

create magnificent sounds and harmonies that the gods never have heard before.

Humans are good at making, create music.

The god of gods then also teaches the human to dance.

Humans enjoy music and danse provided by the handsome god.

For the handsome god, humans have to get rid of his animal side with music, danse, when humans develop creativity.

The handsome god wants humans to upgrade, to improve.

The handsome god tries to do something special with humans.

It's as if, in the universe, it's arid and harsh with no entertainment, battles and wars, but no music, no fun, no entertainment.

Humans are capable of great musical prowess and everything related to creativity, painting, sculpture, arts in general, humans are very good and the king of the gods saw that in humans.

The handsome god is called Apollo among the Greeks and he is the one who promulgates the arts, music, dance, spectacle, poetry, philosophy.

In fact, much like humans are very good in love, humans are naturally very good in creation, creativity.

The other animals on our planet are incapable of creation. The gods are capable of it since the handsome god, the king of the gods, taught humans the flute and the harp as well as the dance, but, once again, humans really seem better on this ground than the gods, on artistic creativity, art, music, dance.

In their travels, their world tours, the gods teach all humans they meet the use of instruments to make music, especially the flute and the harp and a variant that we know very well today.

In India, legends speak of the very beautiful black-haired woman, the goddess Parvati, bringing to the Indians a new string instrument derived from the harp.

She is drawn with this instrument that she invented and gives to humans in India.

A string instrument that the Indians call SITAR and which is the ancestor of the guitar.

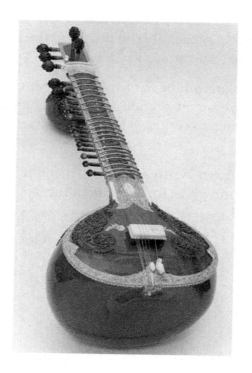

Thousands of miles from India, in Mali, Senegal, Gambia and Guinea, in West Africa, humans use the same ancestral instrument as in India, this stringed instrument is called KORA.

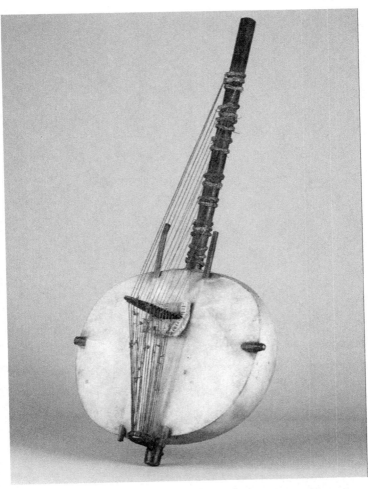

Same shape, with strings, similar to Sitar in India.

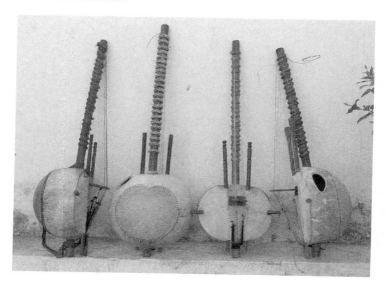

A stringed instrument between the guitar and the harp.

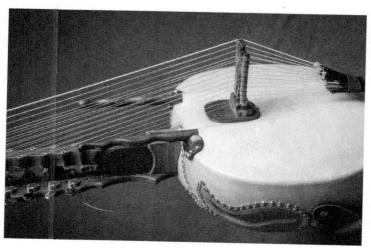

and that Africans have been using for thousands of years also in their rites.

It is amazing that such distant peoples can use the same stringed instrument for so long. Each of these peoples, the Indian people and the Malian people have safeguarded this present of the gods of a distant past.

In India, the great black-haired goddess, called

Parvati, is drawn with this instrument in her hands.

In Africa, legend tells the KORA is the personal instrument of a female genius, a goddess, who appeared in the caves of Missirikoro in Mali.

CHAPTER 17

The gods under attack

The life of these aliens in the universe seems to be difficult and not very fun. They have technological and powerful weapons. The king of the gods, the handsome god, the perfect being, is a very powerful warrior, the most powerful of all the other gods and yet he proves to be the one who believes the most in humans, the one who is kindest and the most compassionate with humans.

The one who is the most generous with humans. The one who forgives humans their animal faults because he sees something special in humans that he has never seen in the universe.

The gods have decided to be kind with humans they like very much. They helped humans and their leader, the king of the gods, get trouble.

For quite a long time, between -6000 BC when they arrived on Earth and -3000 BC, with the gods on Earth helping all people on this planet to live better, to heal themselves with plants, having fun with music, dancing, the arts, living in harmony with the gods made the Earth a true paradise. There is this story of Adam and Eve. Adam is the handsome god, the king of the gods, Eve is this woman goddess with black and long hair. It is written that humans look like them. The tree represents the knowledge that the beautiful god gives to humans. But, as it says in this legend, higher forces, superior beings, did not agree with Adam and Eve so enemies were sent to Earth to destroy the gods and annihilate knowledge.

A first attack of higher forces in the universe was launched and humanoid giants came to fight the gods. These giants, called titans, failed and lost the battle. The gods on Earth were victorious.

Then, the higher forces, superior beings, in the universe, sent even stronger and all the gods on Earth were slaughtered. All gods killed. This is why we find everywhere on Earth ancient gigantic monuments made of huge blocks of stones assembled on top of each other in a technology and a technique that is not ours.

All over Earth, the gods tried to hide and protect themselves against these enemies sent to exterminate them. But, that was not enough and there remain only the ruins of their civilization much more advanced than ours today.

The mighty and magnificent god of gods, the supreme being, the perfect being, the handsome god, generous to humans, has been killed too.

These higher forces also tried to eliminate humans and the knowledge of the gods given to humans.

All the legends around the world speak of a worldwide apocalypse, of fire and destruction, of epidemics and desolation, of devastating submersive waves, of the night that lasted two years preventing agriculture and creating famine in the whole world.

But, these superior forces have minimized the adaptive capacities of humans.

Even though much of the world's population was decimated, humans, hiding in caves, survived all over the world.

After two years in hiding, the devastating superior forces returned to their world, the humans came out of the caves and began to live as if with the presence of the gods and even continued to wait for them. Unfortunately, the gods never returned as they were all executed, all killed.

Humans everywhere on Earth began to reproduce what had been taught by the gods and kept the memories of these exceptional and extraordinary beings through the drawings, legends and mythologies that we know today.

Humans, grateful, will keep in memory and perpetuate the image of the king of the gods, the god of the gods, the perfect being, the handsome god, so exceptional, so amazing, so generous towards humans, from 6000 years until today.

This man is called Vishnu and Shiva in India, Amun Ra and Osiris in Egypt, Apollo in Greece, Balder or Thor in Scandinavia, the pure and perfect being in Japan, the god of the sun in America. Everywhere on Earth, from Europe to Oceania, legends speak of this superior man, the handsome god, kind, good and generous with humans.

What a pity that this man who believed so much in humans disappeared.

He will not have seen the tremendous human progress in creation and creativity.

This amazing man, who had taught humans the flute and the harp will not have seen the rise of classical music, opera, rock, jazz, rap, electronic music and all modern music declined in a myriad of themes.

The handsome god, who had taught humans to dance, will not see all these multitudes of dances invented by humans in history.

As he had expected, humans are really good for creativity in all areas. Humans have invented fashion which does not exist among the gods.

The gods are all dressed the same, not very original.

We have invented entertainment and cinema which do not exist among the gods.

Life in other star systems must be really, really hard because there are a lot of wars and fights and few happy and fun times. This should be difficult when you have eternal life. No fun, only battles.

The king of the gods was a very powerful warrior and the dark-haired woman was a formidable warrior also in the universe.

However, these two formidable warriors took on humans in sympathy and they even stopped fighting by living closer to humans. They really enjoyed this peace life with humans on this planet to the point of not wanting to leave.

Unfortunately, the King of Gods and all the other gods were killed.

Scandinavian mythology speaks of Ragnarok, the last battle of the gods on Earth which they lost.

The forces sent to Earth were, this time, too strong, too powerful. A real hunt for the gods has been launched on Earth and they have all been decimated, one after the other...

... at least almost all of them, only one woman survived. This woman with long black hair, the one who married the god of gods, the powerful woman warrior who loved humans.

The end.

Soon a next book which will explain more details

about the handsome god on : "Super-man "